Becoming Matriarch

A Journey of Pain and Promise

Within my darkest moments, the entry of my words gave me light.

The following are the fibers of thread that have allowed me to stitch my brokenness back together, to shed light on my life; vignettes of spliced-up becoming.

Author

Jenning C. Medina

PALMETTO
P U B L I S H I N G
Charleston, SC
www.PalmettoPublishing.com

Copyright © 2023 by Jenning C. Medina

All rights reserved

No portion of this book may be reproduced, stored in a retrieval system, or transmitted in any form by any means–electronic, mechanical, photocopy, recording, or other–except for brief quotations in printed reviews, without prior permission of the author.

Paperback ISBN: 979-8-8229-3428-3

Acknowledgements

To God be the glory. If not for spirit, ancestors, ascending masters, and source (whomever you choose to draw your faith and perseverance from) none of this would be possible. To be a Universal Citizen is to profoundly appreciate all the powers that be.

Psalms 46:5 "God is within her; she will not fall; God will help her at break of day."

The continuation of this work could not have been possible without my tribe of women who took turns reading excerpts and offering support and criticism while taking time from their own busy schedules to show up for their sister. Many thanks!

There are no coincidences, and nothing is simply by chance! I cannot express enough thanks to my editor, John "Chance" Acevedo, "When the student is ready the teacher will appear." You were right on time! I was exhausted and if not for your mentoring, bullying, and calling me out on procrastination I honestly don't know if I would have been able to tap back in.

To my supportive and loving family, you are my muses, corner, at times believing in me more than I have believed in myself. Without you, my creative force would be hard-pressed to connect to purpose, and I am eternally grateful.

This book is dedicated to my abuela Catalina Arzola, and my momma Maria Canuelas. May this work serve to heal past, present, and future generations.

A Return to Fourth and Life · 1
   Fourth and Life · 2
   Nuyorquina · 6

Boricualogy 101 with a minor in Nuyorican · · · · · · · · · · · · · · 9
   Jones Act · 10
   Law 53 Gag Law · 11
   The Puerto Rican Diaspora · 12
   Nuyorican · 13

Original Matriarch & Founding Paradigm · · · · · · · · · · · · · 15

Miseducation of Maria Luisa · 21
   Dear Mom · 23

Non-Don Medina · 27
   Street Name: Happy · 28

When the Bough Breaks · 31

Baptism by Fire · 37

God bless the Child · 41
   Circa 1992 · 42
   Jeremiah 29:11 · 43

Mi'Ja · 44
Prince Among Us · 46
Mother, may I? · 48

Doña Medina · 51
A Break at Dawn · 52
It's a New Day · 54
Hustle and Flow · 57
Woman Don't Cry · 59
I am not an I Do · 61
Purge · 63
Death of a Soulmate · 64
Broken Women Syndrome · · · · · · · · · · · · · · · · · · 66
Affirmate! · 67
Remnants of Seed · 68
I am that Woman · 69

CreateHer · 71
LoveHer · 72
TravelHer · 73
The Nerve of Her – Clit * Oh * Hiss · · · · · · · · · · · · · · · · · 74
GossipHer · 75
Spirited Righter · 76

About the Author · 81

A Return to Fourth and Life

And forward!

Fourth and Life

Brooklyn: The world as I knew it.
Sunset Park along the "N" & the" R"
I was born and raised on Fourth and Life
Amongst love and strife
My instructions
Against destruction
Was always,
Child, mind your business, or the needle will get you!
A whisper in your ear
A hand in your pocket
Send you to the store at 7.
Silent prayer for heaven to keep you safe.
While she watched out the window from the fourth floor
A pigeonhole's view while she guarded you.
Fiao
Ghetto Style
My Abuela said to put it in the book.
Even back then credit was the hook.
Dame una docena de huevos, un peso de jamón, y un pan italiano
We played games
Very little shame
On the busy noisy
Street
Red light, Green light,
1-2-3
1-2-3
Mother May I
Steal the bacon!
Tag

Home base is the light pole, you're it.
Playing stickball with a broomstick
Bases were
The stoop
A Light pole
A manhole
Past the third car was a home run
Ah, those days were fun!
We were so young.
At the end of the day
You would silently pray.
Up 4 flights of stairs to heaven or hell
Would there be laughs?
Or, screams?
Nightmares?
Or pretty dreams?
Walking through those streets her hand tightens around mine
Past souls, past corners, past streets, past familiar faces
Hug the corner, the street, the soul!
Hug my tio.
In the frio
He slept on the street.
A bum
Street scum
Toma nene un peso, cómprate algo de comer
Everyday life was hard.
We were the worker ants.
Rush, Rush, Rush, gotta go, gotta go.
About to miss the train, hold the doors.
How many people can fit on a pole?
Lack of oxygen lulling me to sleep.
A movie unravels before my droopy eyes.
Express train to heaven or hell down Fourth and Life

A voice replaces the rumble of the metal snake, "Next stop Fourth and Life."
Through the door, take the giant step to clear the floor.
Past the revolving door up the stairs into Brooklyn's core
Eyes adjusting to the light.
The familiar figure and its never-ending plight.
What's up, kid?
What's up tio?
You gotta a dollah?
No
Always automatic
But I would reach in my pocket systematic
Demons fighting
He would always look up and down the street.
Should he just take more?
Or remember the kid in me.
Pity anger embarrassment
Offended at his persona.
I have some change.
His whole face would change.
Eyes speak of broken dreams and broken hope.
Smile with broken teeth
Results of the dope
A family's whole life coping
No words need be spoken.
A whisper in your ear
Take care of yourself
A hand in your pocket
Here get yourself something to eat.
Try to get off the street.
We part.
Clear our throats.
Odd pair
The bum and his niece so fair

We shift.
Each of us going a different way
In life
In the fading light of day,
Above the horizon of Fourth and Life
Past the familiar soul, past the corner, past the street, and up the stairs to heaven or hell.

Nuyorquina

My culture and history have a lot to do with who I am as a person. I am a Nuyorican. A Nuyorican is a blending of the terms "New York" and "Puerto Rican" and refers to the members or culture of the Puerto Rican located in or around New York State, especially the New York City metropolitan area, or of their descendants (mainly those raised or still living in the New York area).

My roots are buried deep on the island of Puerto Rico. I come from Warriors, Guerreras, Tainas. I take great pride in the fact that as diluted as it might be, the blood of a peaceful warrior who welcomed the enemy, runs within my veins.

The Tainos would later revolt against oppression and tyranny and eventually be mutilated and wiped out to become extinct. The Taino Indians worshiped nature and held their ancestors in reverence before Christianity was introduced by the Spanish. My faith is Universe-based, with great respect for the prophets that have impacted our spirits.

This is the groundwork on which the foundation of my being was sewn.

My great-grandfather was Juan Arzola, a "Borinqueneer". He was a member of the 65th Infantry Regiment of the US Army, comprised primarily of Puerto Ricans. Within my matrix lies an ethic, nobility, and strength that has embedded itself into the very nature of our family tree.

I am the great-granddaughter of a soldier. The Borinqueneers would later be recognized for their excellence in service to the United States of America. The regiment's motto is "Honor et Fidelitas", Latin for Honor and Fidelity.

Not too shabby for a colony state. I mean, an unincorporated territory. I mean a commonwealth. I mean, really who wouldn't be confused as to what Puerto Ricans are relative to the U S of A if the island finds it must become politically correct in how it's referenced with every legislative piece that has been issued on its behalf?

Suffice it to say we are a people with a rich history that America had nothing to do with, they found us WHOLE. However, every new administration and generation has tried to whitewash our culture, nature, and our island. They are just waiting in the wings, hoping we forget the hard-to-find travesties in their history books and version of our story.

Boricualogy 101 with a minor in Nuyorican

Jones Act

President Woodrow Wilson signed the Jones-Shafroth Act (1917) on March 2, 1917, giving Puerto Ricans U.S. statutory citizenship. This act also separated Puerto Rico's government into Executive, Judicial, and Legislative branches, and endowed Puerto Ricans with a bill of rights.

Puerto Ricans may enlist in the U.S. military. Since 1917, Puerto Ricans have been included in the compulsory draft whenever it has been in effect and more than 400,000 Puerto Ricans have served in the United States Armed Forces.

As citizens, Puerto Ricans could now join the U.S. Army, but few chose to do so. After Wilson signed a compulsory military service act two months later, however, 20,000 Puerto Ricans were eventually drafted to serve during World War I.

Law 53 Gag Law

Law 53 of 1948 better known as the Gag Law, (Spanish: Ley de La Mordaza) was an act enacted by the Puerto Rico legislature of 1948, to suppress the independence movement in Puerto Rico. The act made it a crime to own or display a Puerto Rican flag, sing a patriotic tune, speak, or write of independence, meet with anyone, or hold any assembly in favor of Puerto Rican independence.

The Puerto Rican Diaspora

At present, the Puerto Ricans are a diasporic people. The increase in the Puerto Rican population on the continent happened simultaneously with an absolute decrease in the population of the Island. With the largest total population as of 2019 being 3,193,694 in PR and 5,828,706 in the US.

I will stop here and simply end this conversational piece, calling it as much, because Puerto Rico has a depth of history that deserves to be front and center, and all on its own. I will point out that since 1898 following the Spanish-American War Puerto Rico has been "the oldest colony in the modern world".

The plethora of Puerto Rican history is what books are made for but not this one.

Part of my journey has been to identify my roots and perhaps your journey, outside of first reading my book, is to acquaint yourself with our history, take a deep dive, and understand why we are so proud of who we are and where we come from.

Nuyorican

I sprouted from a concrete jungle.
Watered into existence by sugar cane hopes and dreams.
Tracing ancestry through the diaspora of a Domino effect, stolen Capicu.

A Brooklyn fourth-floor walk-up bore me on its back.
As I climbed and suckled off the American dream trap!

Social economic development included Bodega credit.
Black and white composition books where our bean counters, Senor Boletero,
Apuntaba hasta el fin del mes. Abuela had an 800-credit score.

¡Porque el que no debe no teme!

The only person I owe anything to is myself!

Constantly on my grind, in pursuit of happiness and independence.
A day one Darwin's daughter pronounced Pedro Albizu Campos "Que viva la Raza".

Born to an environment where only the strong survive. Relentlessly adapting to the beat of my timbal.

How I step matters not. We can do it on one or we can do it on two.
We invented this shit, and the rules don't apply to Us.

Bomba, Danza, Plena – Salsa Salsa Salsa, ¡Reggaeton!

Soy Sandunguera de las primeras.
My pronoun is We!
Enunciated Her Majesty.

Una Taina como de los tiempos de antes cuando la mujer tenía que ser hecha y derecha.

The ones that have, only, ever known "Level up y ponte Vicks Pendeja" and like our resilient island palm trees we bend but we don't break, and this is what you get when you plant Boricuas in concrete.

A flowing multitude of hybrid beautifully engineered perfect DNA that is supported by strong material that bends but will never break.

Original Matriarch & Founding Paradigm

It takes a 'hood to raise a Guerrera; issa village.

I was raised in a hood that had gang violence and high crime, where boarded-up buildings with portraits of flowers on plywood covered the shattered glass windows and you just didn't walk up certain blocks and avenues. My Uncle was like a piece of old black gum stuck on cement; people knew him for being a violent bum affiliated with no one. My Abuela was that mother who hunted him down under the B.Q.E and alleys of those abandoned buildings.

She would walk up to the captain and soldiers of the neighborhood gang and ask over her son "Oye Papi como estas? ¿Como está la familia? ¿Mira viste a Junior hoy? Bendito nene cocine y quiero que venga a comer. Si lo ves dile que se vaya a la casa!" all the while tightly gripping my hand as I would go along with her on her hunt to find my uncle.

They would respond "No Ma pero si lo veo le digo" She was never afraid and would gently touch an arm or shoulder ready to give her blessing "Ok Nene que Dios te bendiga" the hardened soul from the hood would bow his head and say "Bendición Mami". My grandmother taught me how to look into the eyes of the beast and find their hearts. My uncle might have had street credibility for giving no fucks over human life, a person like that is to be feared because they have nothing to lose. My Grandmother had hood love and respect. She was the one who hunted her kids down in fear of nothing and no one. That's respect!

She loved to dance and socialize. One of her nicknames was 'Buelita Merengue'. Every female that is a descendant of this woman enjoys "El bembe".

She'd party in Brooklyn, hitting the local joints, where they served the mini- Budweiser's. In the game until her late 70's - every Friday at the salon. After the novela finished, she'd start her makeup, and draw in the eyebrows, perfect eyebrows have always been a thing. Once the makeup was on, she'd get at that rotary phone gently spraying aqua net finishing on the hair color of the week, Penny color was her favorite "pa' tapar las canas".

"Esther cuando llegues, subeme una cervecita de la bodega te doy los tres pesos cuando llegues" some Avon perfume would get sprayed on and a stick of Juicy Fruit bubble gum would get released from its aluminum foil and popped into her mouth. Ritual.

When I think of Abuela I think in scents; the bacalao y vianda she always had ready for me when I came to visit because she knew it was my favorite dish.

She cleaned her home with King Pine and Clorox "Nena no importa si tienes trapos como furnitura lo que importa es que este limpio" Cleanliness was next to godliness. She believed that no matter what possessions you had, cheap or couture, the value was in how you took care of it.

Vicks and alcoholado for those days I fell ill (I suffered from anemia as a child) and the healing practice for my sick days were alcohalado doused towels that she would wrap around my head, a slab of Vicks on my chest no matter what I was suffering, accompanied by sopa de leche, her version of food for the soul. But not before she was shoving a hefty spoon of Emulsion de Scott (fish oil) down my throat while pulling at my lower eyelids to examine the inside skin "tu necesita vitaminas."

Abuela was my northern star. Her advice in its simplicity would always put me on my path,

Her words echo "Tu haz lo que tenga que hacer para tu felicidad porque lo de mas es un cuento y si tienes un pensamiento hecha lo por delante." translation "You do what you need to do for your happiness the rest is history and if you have a thought put it into action."

A person like that goes through her becoming, shedding different versions of themselves so that they in turn can become a more refined version of Source!

She landed and rooted herself in the crevices of Sunset Park and raised this neighborhood Nena.

When I was born at Sister Elizabeth Medical Center and sent home, it was to Abuela's home I went to. When my firstborn was born at Lutheran Medical Center and sent home, it was Abuela's home we went home to. She was the cradle of life. I was her baby and although I did not come from her womb, I came from her essence, I basked and grew in the glow of her love. If not for her I know not what my life would have become. I am privileged to call Catalina Arzola Morales my grandmother.

During the greater part of my life, Abuela protected, loved, and guided me. She instilled in me core values that spoke to being a good mother, una mujer hecha y derecha, y siempre una luchadora!

It wasn't all lollipops and cupcakes; she was tough and there was not one person in our family that she did not butt heads with.

For me, the smackdown would go like this:

"Tu si eres una mal cría Jenning"

"Tengo a quien salir Abuela"

"¿O sí? Mírame a mí, sin educación, sin poder hablar español, no sé cómo escribir ni se leer. ¡Pero los ha creado a ustedes, tengo este casco de apartamento y unos cuantos trapos y vivo lo más feliz! ¡Como una Reina! Ustedes que se anido han ido para escuela y a estudiar con toda su educación siempre terminan aquí con esta vieja tratando de decir me a mi como vivir."

"Tienes razón Abuela es verdad."

"Pues cogelo con take it easy baby y cállate you mouth."

I would shut up! She served you humble pie con pan Italiano y un huevo frito.

If I close my eyes, I hear her from the living room once I've walked into the apartment after being absent for a couple of weeks.

"Resucitaste Nena?"

"Bendición Abuela."

"Que Dios te bendiga Nena!"

If I close my eyes I can hear her say;

"Pareces que no estas sufriendo porque esta seba de gorda!"

If I open my heart her words echo in my spirit.

"Nena la salud es lo más importante en la vida porque sin la salud no se puede hacer nada!"

She was a prayer warrior who taught me how to pray not in theory but in application. On her knees at the beginning of my life and much later, as she lay in bed and her knees didn't allow for hard floors, she prayed for her supplications but mostly praise and gratitude for another day and always for the protection of her loved ones. I never heard my grandmother ask God for anything when it came to herself. All she ever asked for was that her family be protected and here we are, her loved ones, protected by her benedictions and her prayers.

If I bow my head I can see all the stairs that lead down from her 4th-floor walkup, she would watch us leave, her eyes following us down to the first floor from her landing, and for every landing, she repeated her bendiciones and her "ten cuidadito por ahi" until you got to the first floor and screamed up to her "Abuela entra" only then would she go into her apartment when she couldn't see you anymore but you knew as she was closing the door behind her, she was whispering to God prayers for your safety – "Ay Padre Celestial cuidamelo".

She is a collective of memories and a whole mood.

Abuela, if nothing more, was a place of refuge, an open door no matter what, from the worst of us to the best of us. She covered us in blessings, the truest form of love. She could feed a multitude on a fixed income and the first person who received money from her check was the homeless bum outside of the check cashing place because "yo tengo un hijo en la calle" her compassion for those that were hit with hard times had no boundaries.

If I stumbled on my journey through life and needed to go back home, I didn't know what shame was, I did, however, feel disappointment.

That sense of letting her down never stopped me from going back home because I knew no matter what her door would be open, and a plate of food would be waiting for me. She would read me and write me while pulling out clean linen to dress the bed that was always available for her family and friends.

"acomódate por ahi como puedas a ver qué es lo que vas hacer."

There have been times when entire sub-families of our family lived in one room in her public housing apartment, my own family included. There was no shame in it! There was only refuge! A place of shelter, not made for comfort but instead for healing. And, as most of us know, there are times in our lives when healing is uncomfortable.

She didn't want people living with her, but my grandmother understood the importance of giving her loved one's cover; she was a refuge with no judgment.

Miseducation of Maria Luisa

Mom and I would go years without speaking to one another. I subscribe to the notion that you should remove yourself from toxic situations and people, even if they are family members. Just because they hold a title in your life does not mean you are a servant to it; you are allowed to leave the relationship.

You own your happiness.

My relationship with my mom had always been toxic. How couldn't it be? Our bond, from inception, was infused in the womb with self-loathing and despair. I do not remember there ever being a time when my mom didn't hate her life.

In her early fifties, she was diagnosed with cancer and like the very cancer she was fighting, our family had been ravaged by disease. A disease that had bred itself into the backbone of our family and it crippled our ability to love one another and to heal. Infighting.

My daughter would be the tool that bridged the gap, she frequently video-chatted with my mother. I didn't come in between that relationship, just because our relationship didn't function well didn't mean she couldn't be a better grandmother to my daughter than she was a mother to me.

During one of those chats, my daughter put me on the spot - "Mommy, Grandma wants to speak with you." I preach from an extremely high pulpit, trying to be the best example I can be, I won't feed cancer, no form of it, especially when it comes to my children. So, I took the call and faced my mother. She immediately broke down crying, as did I. You can either cry over spilled milk or clean it up, this has been my emotional and spiritual journey with my mom, cleaning up trauma. Mine. Hers. Ours.

Lamenting what I never received from her or what she did not freely give me was yet another form of rejection. Rejecting the idea that I could heal this mother wound.

Looking into the face of the woman that I so heavily resembled, I pledged to continue to battle this cancer, the type that goes undiagnosed; it is emotional and convinces us that there is no cure for the unloved. She is a part of my matrix and recognizing this has saved my life.

There is no cure for the unloved, there is only healing.

My mother would transition a few years later, and it was then that my healing, or lack thereof would get tested.

I mourned what I had wanted my entire life and didn't have, and it took me the better part of two years to recognize that Mom and I had never experienced the type of relationship I craved. You don't know what you don't know. So, why? Where did all the suffering come from?

In an attempt to reconcile my grief and suffering, on her born day I wrote her a letter.

Dear Mom,

Your first granddaughter celebrated her Sweet 16 this year. Remember how you would tell her how you could not wait for that day? It was like we were all planning that day for her from the moment we found out I was having a little girl.

This year was tough. I grieved you hard. I suffered from terrible panic and anxiety. On the day of Jocie's Sweet 16 on my way to the hall, I started crying. I remember saying "I wish my mom was here."

Mom, that is when it happened, clarity. My heart wanted something that I had never experienced with you and although I wanted you there, I knew the day would not have turned out the way it did if you were a part of it.

The harsh truth is that you either would not have shown up because of your anxiety, your concern over your physical appearance, and/or a countless number of excuses that would have disappointed Joc but would have made sense to you.

If we had convinced you to be a part of it, we would've had to cater to you and be sensitive to your needs during the entire affair to make you comfortable with your insecurities. It would not have been about my daughter, kids, family, or friends, it would've been about you; Maria.

I took care of you and our family for the better part of my whole life, and I knew at that moment that I had stopped because I was still trying to raise myself while pushing the rest of this family into the world.

I broke this year. I put you on a pedestal, I created an illusion of you that was unrealistic because that had not been our reality.

Happy Birthday, Mom! This year on your behalf I am giving myself clarity. I feel myself coming up from the fog of confusion and pain. I am rising. With that rise comes more love and light. Mom, I love you. May your journey beyond the veil be full of all your family's love and light. We are shining!

Love you always,
Your Firstborn

On the eve of the second anniversary of Mom's transition, I mourned her passing, I intentionally sat with the grief and mourned the should've, would've, and could've. I mourned the unresolved. Our pain sits heavy in my heart. I did not want to repurpose these feelings just to have a sense of healing and closure. I interrogate that we want to celebrate love and life but not face loss and trauma from the same.

As I continue to face and explore my emotions, I have come to the realization that healing is taking place. For an entire year after her passing, I stuffed my emotions and bottlenecked. I was then forced to face my emotions, to feel them in manners that were a repeat of the trauma I had experienced with her, because of her, through her, she was my amniotic fluid. She hard-wired me. She was in me. I am never going to escape those hard facts. What I can prevent is being swallowed whole by her genetic code and legacy. This is not a mythological story in which the Goddess eats her babies because of some prophecy that was foretold that we should all be destroyed because of the ripple effect of circumstance and consequence.

There are no heroes in this story. There are no villains. There is character conflict and there is life! She was born for me, and I was born for her and not every story has a lovely ending. This is not to say we don't share this part of the story. We must. Our survival depends on it.

I'm tracing her steps, I'm climbing the pyramids of her existence, I acknowledge I do not want to be on the same path, but her journey lends me clues to my becoming. Breaking generational curses requires the knowledge of how we arrived at this place.

On the anniversary of her homegoing, I mourn Maria with no resistance to my feelings because in the natural to mourn love is as necessary as it is to celebrate love. I have become okay with my emotions. I am in recognition of mourning voids in my heart space. Vacuums that had always been there, hovering in the peripheral, trying to fit square pegs into round holes. With her loss, I knew without a doubt that another could not fill those voids, except perhaps her daughter; me. Identifying and reconciling these emotions was part of my evolution.

Non-Don Medina

My father died in my early twenties of health complications due to his lifelong struggle with heroin.

When he died, I received a call from my mother during a shift at a topless bar I bartended at where she called me on their public pay phone. The call came through and I could barely hear her amidst all the noise, cheap perfume, and alcohol-induced laughter, drowning out the normal level of conversation, my mother could be heard speaking loudly almost screaming so I could hear her over the craziness "Hello?! Jenning?! Do you hear me? Jenning?! Your father died today" the silence on the other end of the call was deafening "Jenning, did you hear me?" I replied "Yes Mom, I got to go, they're waiting for me at the bar" I ended the call, and I went back to work, and proceeded as if nothing happened.

Street Name: Happy

RIP:
Street Name: Happy
Description: Tecato

On the day of his funeral, I called ahead, wanting to have some privacy to pay my respects. I was granted an hour before public viewing.

I looked at the man to whom I had been ashamed my whole life, an addict who would collect white foam at the edge of his mouth during conversation and fall asleep mid-sentence. The one who would leave me waiting when it was time to get picked up for our weekends together. My mother was a witness to my pain and disappointment, instead of taking me into her arms and loving me through it, she would continually break him down calling him a "drug addict" and saying things like "Why do you even care if he picks you up? He's disgusting!" It broke me down at a cellular level. It didn't matter what he was, I was his daughter, and his failures as a father planted themselves in my spirit. Shame. For the better part of my life, I was ashamed to be the daughter of a heroin drug addict.

Viewing the frozen body, I had no sense of connection to the man I had called Daddy, so I squeezed my eyes tight and forced myself to remember that this very man took care of me as a newborn when my mom went through a post-partum mental break down and left me with him, I was but days old and yet he took care of me. I continued staring into the darkness of my mind's eyes and squeezed out memories of the times when he was clean from his addiction and would take me for Ice Cream while he played his numbers, proudly show me off, and say "This is my little girl. Jenning, mami, what do you want? Pick whatever you want."

Opening my eyes and looking down at the frozen mask of a man who was no longer present and chained to his body. I finally started crying, the shame of having an addict for a father spilled out hot, an acid that poured over festering wounds, it was then that I understood I had also been ashamed of myself.

Although I made peace with my father once he passed away, I was heavily affected by his lack of presence while growing up, I suffered the absence of his protection. I questioned his love and when I did get a chance to spend time with him I questioned his role as a father, he would point to a tattoo on his arm of baby Pebbles from the Flintstones with my name under it and say "Mami, every time I look into the mirror and I see your name I think of you, every day, you are a permanent part of my skin" as if that was enough of a justification to checking out of his responsibilities and leaving me unprotected.

On many a heart-in-throat, grief-stricken night, I needed him to save me, to tuck me in, give me forehead kisses, and help me rebuke and bind devils.

Instead, he was tucking himself into a heroine-induced haze while his little girl was being tucked in by her mother's boyfriend and wandering hands. Hands that roamed over the undeveloped body parts of this little girl and marked her forever. What is innocence? I wasn't allowed to keep mine.

Every failed relationship has triggered my daddy issues and the profound feeling of abandonment. Every failed attempt, in that a man is unable to properly protect me or love me and leaves me, is reminiscent of weekends when I was left waiting for the man chosen to protect me but instead deserted me.

Rejection has left me with my own track lines.

When the Bough Breaks

> "Someone I loved once gave me a box full of darkness. It took me years to understand that this too, was a gift." - Mary Oliver

My parents receive no special accolades. What they do receive are awards for best practices on how to screw your kid up emotionally, mentally, spiritually, and physically.

Mother's Day and Father's Day hallmark cards screamed hypocrisy and the proximity between the two dates turned me into an emotional sandwich.

If there were times my mother and I did acknowledge Mother's Day, it would normally come in guilt-laden communication.

"I'm sorry you hate me; I did the best I could with what I knew." In my eyes, once my mother attended college and exposed herself to a higher level of education, that excuse went out the door and so did her platitude for victimization.

Her major was Early Childhood Education, and yet she never fully understood that my inner child needed her to mother me. Instead, because of her title as my mother I should reverie her.

"Jenning, you only get one mother. You should honor me."

I never just had one mother, every woman who became a mentor in my life, every woman who attached themselves to my journey and nurtured and loved me became my mother.

"I hope your kids never treat you the way you treat me." They try and I try even harder to understand and become a better mother. Some days even that's not enough.

"One day you will know how this feels Mamita. God bless you." She always left me with a bitter aftertaste when she projected wanting me to go through the same trials and tribulations as she did just so I could "feel" her experience she would end her tirades with "God bless you."

As a single mother, I have incorporated the lessons passed down to me by my father, mother, grandmother, and social environment. They have been a study of "dos and don'ts"! A manual to reference during the good, bad, ugly, and triumphant journey of becoming.

Our family is not exempt from the experiences that have plagued many a family but who you become in the wilderness determines how effective the enemy will be in your life. I was raised by The Original Matriarch in a concrete jungle born into an inhospitable environment.

I never crowned. I breached. Tentacles of nourishment trying to strangle my life. I fought to come through, purple in the face, the color of royalty. I was freed the moment they cut the cord. My first breath was a ROAR! I was placed into my robes with purpose and destiny. Never assuming majesty, the struggle for my sovereignty has been earned, building stability, and grounding myself in faith. From this One life came four. I have multiplied. I've been counted out, underestimated, and odds stacked against me from the beginning. I am not one statistic, I am MANY!

When this physical world fails me, I just sit back and allow the powers that be, my ancestors, those who delivered me into this realm against all odds to do what is done best, manifest.

While I get into my feelings when my inner child gets triggered and relives trauma, I am grateful for not having turned into a basket case. There are stages in my life that were a train wreck, choices, and decisions that faint hearts don't bounce back from, yet here I am picking up pieces of myself from the rubble.

Parenthood doesn't come with a manual and to add insult to injury, some of us come from upbringings that are saturated in trauma and crisis, we fall into the same cycles with our children because that is all we know, that is our comfort zone. Crisis. Kudos to the parents who are doing the work necessary to heal their inner child as well as their children.

Not recognizing I have my parent's mental health challenges is like not claiming my dad's brown eyes or my mom's beautifully sculpted cheekbones. Knowing is half the battle. It's all part of the matrix and biology! I'm grateful for their experiences, for it has better prepared me for my becoming. My Father used heroin to escape, and my mother turned to prescription drugs to solve her insomnia, depression, and anxiety. Couple that with trauma, and it's a mixed bag.

Blessed be the veil has lifted. I'm in acknowledgment.

As much as I would love to talk about organic or best health practices and clean eating, the very nature of science has muddied the waters. We have been altered for preventative methods that immunize us against disease, live within polluted environments, and consume genetically modified organisms. Add genetic correlation and a nested structure of hereditary evaluation. We are not so organic a human race.

It must be with a committed heart and a conscious effort that we endeavor to find the balance between birth and becoming. How we practice will affect future generations. We heal ourselves through thoughts, intentions, and sound healthy practices.

As I move into researching methods that assist me with my health challenges, specifically Fibromyalgia, I focus on methods that concentrate on holistic approaches and minimize my use of pharmaceuticals. Did not the very use of "drugs" modify my parents and in turn myself? I can see where my family biology suffers from serotonin and dopamine deficiencies. We stay wanting a fix; a high.

You can be genetically wired to suffer deficiencies. You can have your Momma's eyes and her tendencies of depression while having your Daddy's anxieties and his curly hair.

Genetics correlates with everything. I can trace back generations and generations of mental unhealth. We want to try to keep things simple; exercise, eat right, meditate, and boom problem solved but we fail to grasp how intricate a creation we truly are.

Don't get me wrong, those things are super important but if you find yourself in a cycle even still while implementing those things don't give up and don't judge yourself, there are greater forces in place; your natural state of being.

As I peel away the onion and dissect my genetics on a cellular level, I am grateful for the awareness and the acknowledgment. I am healing my family's history by giving it color and understanding while eliminating judgment. I am creating a knowledge base, documenting resources, and communicating the journey to my children so they may be equally if not better prepared for their reference.

Often accused of overthinking, of being too deep, if I've learned anything is that one must mine for strength and alchemize those uncomfortable moments to create a journey of perseverance. I come from mental and emotional bankruptcy, and it has affected every aspect of my upbringing and well-being, so much so that early on it affected my parenting. The damage is done. The behavior has been modified; I've become a better Mom for it. I will continue to grow, to change, to seek awareness. Not so much for myself but because I'm persistently building equity from a mental health perspective so that my children and their children can have the means necessary to approach all facets of their lives with more balance.

People are constantly reinforcing how strong I am. I appreciate you. If I could give you a glimpse of what my everyday looks like, this is it. It takes a lot of mental strength and resolution to get up every day and shadowbox. We are only ever fighting ourselves.

Baptism by Fire

I was meant to pass through the fire. It purified me. I am a second-generation single mother. My grandmother was a single mother, my mom was a single mother, and I am a single mother. This was the standard we fell in; this is the pattern in which we were raised.

My grandmother left an abusive husband. A sick man whose DNA included abuse, lunacy, and addiction. This genetic material would seed its self-destructive mechanisms into future generations. She made her mistakes with her children and during her later years tried to hold for her family as best she could with her limited education and lack of mental health comprehension.

My Mother was the first of her generation to graduate college with a bachelor's degree in early childhood education while raising her children. My Mother was sexually abused as a young teenager, a high school dropout, who became pregnant at 16 by my much older father and was forced to marry him to save face. She would experience a life of suffering. I have learned you can stash away nightmares and temporarily lock away your demons, but unresolved trauma has an expiration date.

My mother would move on through life accomplishing and sabotaging. She and I had a love/distaste relationship. How do you genuinely love the child of a man whom you were forced to marry? How do you love wholeheartedly if your definition of love is distorted? I represented trauma in her life.

It is now my turn to raise the next generation. As I move into the fall and winter of my life and the idealistic layers roll off me like dead skin I understand the lunacy, the pain and suffering, the expiration dates of locked-away trauma, depression, anxiety, causal DNA, and the environments that had so much to do with our trauma.

These are my women. To deny the generations before me and say I am different is to completely deny ME! You get a blueprint and then you get choices that dictate how you are going to build with the material you have been given. I am building and it is painstakingly intentional.

It is the materialization of my every trauma and every oppression. My body will not hold on to it anymore! It refuses to ignore and listen to yet another:

"You're strong, Jenning."

"You're a warrior, Jenning."

"You got this, Jenning."

Although I am all those things, I would not have had to be those things my WHOLE life if there wasn't a reason for it.

We are not built, as human beings, to be under constant stress. Do you know what happens to us as we experience trauma? We may encounter PTS (Post Traumatic Syndrome), an often-adaptive response to experiencing a traumatic or stressful event. Now, apply that to a lifetime. Exactly what does the evolution of such a life look like? You are reading about her.

You don't know what you don't know, until one day you experience such a bad panic attack it feels like you're having a heart attack or you're in so much physical pain that you can't help but go into a fetal position, it is utterly exhausting, and you hear your mother's voice in your head "I'm in pain every day, Jay. I hope you never have to go through this." I knew secretly she needed someone to "feel" her pain. She chose me. She. Choose. Me.

The physical symptoms I experience when under duress are indicators of a life lived under constant stress and trauma. They will not be shelved, a mishap or an experience quaintly cataloged in words that become painful prose. They will be felt. They are shaking me down. I have gone through very painful physical transitions. No less traumatic than the birthing pain of yesteryears. Every cycle and every becoming have brought with it a symptom to be added to this list.

Once my mother transitioned, I went into a phase that I like to think of as "Healing the Mother Womb," connecting to my mother's pain trying to trace her steps yet not wanting to go through the same journey. She lacked Oneness, connection, and synchronicity.

Here I am a self-proclaimed family disease detective applying what I have learned along the way. Determined to thrive instead of just surviving trauma and crisis.

God bless the Child

Circa 1992

I was born to a Sixteen-year-old.
He was born to a Seventeen-year-old.
We were firstborns who cut our teeth on underdeveloped mothers' milk. We latched on to trauma, chaos, and distorted love.
Many lessons have curdled while we've been forced to digest hurt, pain, and despair.
Yet, what we've been able to hold down has been enough to cast aside deficient placenta.
Under the cradle cap lay crowns.
Kings come from Queens.

Jeremiah 29:11

"For I know the plans I have for you."

My second son is the most spiritual of the four. The prayer warrior and the seeker of the way maker. Surely God understood I needed a spiritually rooted soul to accompany me on this journey. The Most High knew the plans he had for this family.

Jeremy is our spiritual lynchpin.

He is a firm believer that "Love wins every time." And it does!

Mi'Ja

My daughter, how do I teach you what you need to know if everything that you must learn is contrary to what I was taught, by my mother and grandmother and what they defined as "Woman" or "Una mujer echa y derecha." To cook, clean, raise your children; take care of your husband, work like a man, pursue education, eat, sleep, and repeat. At no cost to your sanity, health, heart, spirit, or soul.

How do I teach you to love yourself? That you must come first, second, and third. Never questioning how good a love you give because it comes from a generous fountain, consistently replenished from within.

How do I teach you not to forget yourself? Affirming and connecting to ancestry. You come from a finely fused line of Guerreras, Exclaves, y Conquistadores. I dare say a more contrary concoction of femininity you may never find, Mujeres who laid down their weapons at the first sign of partnership to not affect the balance of so unequally divided Herstory.

How do I teach you that you should not lay down anything until you've been raised so high that surely you must have met Obatala himself and you're sitting on the highest Loma looking down at the world, a pearl at your feet? You are not a Queen, eres una Diosa, Grandiosa.

Many a kingdom lay plundered baby, banners flapping in the wind whispering defeat, vultures crying "Matriarch," no sign of a Shining Armor for so easy a booty, cupid arrow holes riddled hearts all because of the promise of partnership. 50/50 is not 100% it is still half. Don't get fooled by simpleton math. A glass half full may quench your thirst but it will never feed the fires of your ambition. I swallowed ambition like a forbidden fruit and gave birth to a hybrid generation. You!

How do I teach you to master your carnal desires in order to be a student of connection?!

In a society where everything comes in short-span distractions and superficial ego-tripping, how do I teach you to focus? To mine for longevity. How do I teach you to hold out, rock steady, and either he will break himself against you or cover you with paper.

How do I teach you to fight for boundaries yet be a mediator of compromise?

Ay Mija, anything with two heads is a monster, so how do I teach you to concede, to take a step back not because you are less worthy of being a leader but because a true leader leads from the back?

But first, how do I teach you to love yourself when everything that you must learn is contrary?

Prince Among Us

Peter, my youngest child, has received the best version of mother that I can offer to date. His older siblings have molded me, taught me, and developed me. At times, the lessons have been jarring and harsh.

During the earlier stages of motherhood, I took so much for granted, rushing through life with blinders on. Missing the formative years to give them the future I thought they needed.

Peter is the last of the line and as such I have tried to be as present as possible, absorbing every moment of every second. While still trying to have enough grace with myself and acknowledging that each child has had a different version of me as a parent, experiencing my development amidst their growth.

Peter is a product of a self-actualized single Mother. In lending himself to my journey he became a different approach to parenting, the cornerstone of the structure of my current life, unknowingly assisting me back to self as I transitioned and took ownership of my process as a woman and mother.

Everything I have done has been to create an energetic field that he could thrive in, thereby creating a vibration they all connect to. He is our beloved.

As far back as I can remember when I was asked what I wanted to be in life, I always responded "A Mother". I have traded my soul at times to be a mother. Horrifying. Selfish. Ignorant. They say hindsight is 20/20. As I do this work, this spiritual work, I am in the realization of my selfishness.

Why?

Certainly because of the circumstances in which I delivered my children into this dimension. By hook or crook my soulmates were going to come through. I needed them, wanted them here with me. Ready or not!

We handpicked each other, dragging each other along our respective journeys. Periodically questioning our choices. We have and continue to explore all the emotions that come along with being biologically bound to a human being.

Imperfection is a motherfucker! We have not been the best of friends but there is an invisible thread that binds us and can never be severed. We are in this!

I get this a lot, "OH MY GOD, you have FOUR kids?" Yes!

They each have a story. Like elementals. They each have a purpose. Recently I had someone exclaim over the number of children I have, and I responded "Yes, at one point I wanted to populate the world " and laughed it off, she responded, quite seriously "If anyone is going to populate the world, I'm glad it's you" my purpose has always been and every day of my life; my children, my family. Anyone who is a witness to my becoming can easily attest to this.

They are purpose, they are life. I am them. They are me. We are ONENESS. We are family.

Mother, may I?

Do you realize how important you are?

Where your value lies?

What you represent in the grand scheme of things?

A biblical passage comes to mind and speaks itself into my meditative space.

John 14:6 Jesus answered, "I am the way and the truth and the life. No one comes to the Father except through me."

If Father is God, and Mother and Father are synonyms of one another, where do you think I'm going with this?

It may be a bit sacrilegious to call you Goddess because a Goddess has always been related to paganism but if Jesus Christ is the way, the truth, and the life and no one can get to the Father except through him I'm going to fall on the sword and say "Humanity cannot get to the Son if it does not first come through the Mother; Goddess."

Muslims believe that a unique connection exists between God and the womb. Through the womb, you get a glimpse of the Almighty's qualities and attributes. It nurtures, feeds, and shelters us in the early stages of life. The womb can be viewed as one manifestation of divinity in the world: a connection to the divine.

Do you grasp how sacred a vessel you are?

When you call mothering/parenting "Work" you belittle your role, this is not an occupation dear one this is your partnership with God. Sacrifices speak to a loss, you "give" birth, if you have lost anything it is comprehension. My favorite one is "Thankless Job" In truth it makes me want to cry because I've seen the face of God, in my children. They incubated in a place so sacred and divine that surely it must be paradise. There is nothing thankless about divinity. My children don't validate me; my partnership is with God, he validated me when he favored me with children.

If you're a single mother who in your opinion procreated with a "Deadbeat Dad" be careful in what you speak into your child's spirit. Trust me when I tell you that children absorb all our hurt, pain, and worthlessness. Worthlessness that is relatable with being connected to a "Deadbeat Dad". DNA is an identifier, you can't erase identity, don't further cripple your child by creating a cancer in their identity that will eat away at them. Speak life into them not death.

A Mother's heart is an extension of the womb, for once the womb has done its job the heart will sustain you for life.

What is a mother really? You are the vast Universe that incubates atoms and Adams giving birth to the world, a vessel that is the channel to the beginning and the end, the gatekeeper, and through you hope is born into the world. Life is dependent on you as much as Saviors and Prophets. Step into your divinity, you are the "I am that I am, Mother".

Doña Medina

A Break at Dawn

Every new day is an opportunity to be born again and dig deep within yourself, plant your intentions, and nurture yourself.

Essentially, it is a call to spiritual renewal. To recommit yourself and be grateful to have an opportunity to go at life again, and again. Some days it is an exercise in "taking the first step even when we don't see the whole staircase."

In my semi-woke state, I tried focusing on a comforting scene, pulling up a visual of a Saturday spent in gently worn flannel pajamas, a house sweater, and a cup of smoldering peppermint tea while curled up on the couch watching marathons of Law and Order.

I took a deep breath and let the sadness wash over me, wanting to release it, needing it to let go of my weary soul. My brain echoed despair. Tired. I was so tired.

Having tucked myself into a cocoon of suffering the night before, I felt emotionally drained and terribly vulnerable.

The pain I had been experiencing lately had nothing to do with the heartbreak you attribute to a failed relationship. Although it was a matter of the heart it was not the type you would lay at a man's feet. Living life wholeheartedly and loving it deeply will sometimes drain you just as badly as a disappointing love affair. No, this was not a romantic breakup, this was a life shakedown, and some days life was an angry sea of never-ending waves, furiously pummeling the shit out of you.

Crawling into bed, soul tired, emotionally exhausted I had dissolved into tears. Craving the strong arms of a life partner, wanting the strength of someone stronger than me to absorb my pain, hold me, rub my back, lend me the rhythm of their heart so that I could hear its beat and remember what it was to breathe.

Submerged in darkness, alone in my bed, with just my thoughts, wondering "If we were meant to be alone, we wouldn't come into the world attached to another human being" I no longer bought into the idea of finding "Self" first - I wasn't born alone. I craved to be connected. I raged, asking myself "Where is the womb of love that will provide me a safe harbor?" I had not created myself. I hungered for the amniotic fluid that doubled as a hug and silently screamed into the darkest of nights "Come! Where the fuck are you?!"

Yet here I lay, having survived another night of this beautiful thing called "Life". Quietly waiting for the alarm to do its job because yet again I had woken up before 6 a.m. and the sound of chimes had not struck a chord. A slight headache reminded me that I had shrouded myself in tears the night before.

Lying still in meditation, I prayed and received the day while practicing my breathing.

There had been a time when I would wake up with a racing heart and an overactive nervous system, learning to recognize anxiety and panic has been a lifetime journey of self-discovery.

Mental health has been a dark specter in my family, an unwanted family member, attaching itself to every generation for as far back as I can remember.

To have an effective journey of self-discovery I have had to peel the onion and go back to the very root of the disease and in doing so I have realized that while I may have created some of my trauma, I was not the creator of all of it. La sangre llama.

It's a New Day

The sound of chimes for a 6 am alarm softly rings and we are off to the races.

I gently call out "Peter" my body popping and cracking into place as I swing my legs off the bed and shy away from hardwood floors that have no mercy in the winter. My feet blindly look for my chancletas. My ankle snapped, my knee popped, and my shoulder cracked. I feel like a Kellogg's commercial. Midlife body sucked and there was absolutely nothing sexy about sounding like a cold cereal jingle while trying to get out of bed!

"Peter!"

"Yes, Momma. I'm up. Can I stretch for two minutes?" Procrastination is real.

My mornings pretty much started in the same fashion.

We had perfected our morning routine to under an hour; breakfast, shower, hair, makeup, packing lunches and snacks, while trying to have very minimal wardrobe mishaps because depending on the day one could feel fabulous, skinny, bloated, ugly, pretty, grey, or colorful and your choices depended on your mood; pantsuit with pumps, pencil skirt (being a curvaceous Latina it was a sharpie skirt for me – I made a permanent statement) with a thick heel, dress with sandals or boots depending on the weather, black skinny jeans that could pass for office casual if you wore the right top, blazer, and shoes.

The damn combinations could be limitless as well as the freaking moods. A woman's closet should be organized by hormonal phases.

Of course, every day brought with it a different challenge, and most of the mornings I was a hot-mess mom who was trying to get out of the house on time and was beating a path between my bedroom and the bathroom while barking orders to Peter from a mouth-foaming of toothpaste and dripping of mouthwash.

"Do I owe you any money for school trips, donations, or just extra crap in general?"

He would flip through his "take home folder" weeding out old tests, notices, homework, and permission slips shaking his head "No. We're good."

Simultaneously swishing and spitting out the last of my mouthwash I yell "Time check?"

To make him responsible for the time we walk out the door, I implemented a time check system. We kept each other on the move.

Pressing the home button on his iPad he turned and walked briskly to his room, barking "7 a.m. – if we don't leave now, we'll run late." Grabbing his backpack, pulling on his jacket, and walking towards the front door he yells. "Let's go!"

Through the years, walking into my shoes, throwing on my scarf, pulling on my jacket, and grabbing my tote, purse, cellphone, and car keys had turned into a bionic move. If the average person blinks twice, they will miss it. We were out!

Hustling down the stairs, rapidly walking to the car, throwing my weighed-down tote and purse onto the front seat, sliding into the driver's seat, glancing into the rearview mirror to make sure a kid was in the car and buckled in was mechanical, a routine, it was our life, and we had perfected it. It also had me constantly wondering if the whole exercise counted as fasted cardio because can a thick chick lose a pound or two while going through life with such consistency and dedication? Cycling class got nothing on a single mother doing this damn thing.

My kid was asleep before my Pandora stations had connected to Bluetooth. He always fell asleep in the car. Peter suffered from motion sickness and coped by putting himself to sleep. It was a twelve-minute ride to his school. At red lights, I'd sneak peeks of him in the rearview mirror taking turns praying and thanking God for another day of health, life, love, family, friends, opportunity, and no traffic. Pretty much in that order.

I'd put four kids through the same school of practice. Four children of drop-offs, pickups, sports, work, home, and repeat.

By the time you read this book, I would have been a mother for 31 years and that is not counting the responsibility I had over my younger siblings. There was no other recourse but to perfect this process. Some days you get to work with stains on your clothes, a kid missing trip money, a nurse calling you after you just dropped said kid off with your kid complaining of a stomachache that materialized out of nowhere, or you leave your wallet at home, or the bus is running an hour late, or how about the time your kid gets suspended for burning a Capri Sun juice box straw at lunch and became a menace to society, the list goes on.

The academic life of my children and their shenanigans got Diary of a Wimpy Kid beat!

Most of our days were just a brilliantly choreographed shit show.

Hustle and Flow

My hour-and-a-half-long commute to the office is a test of my patience. I am a slave to seconds and minutes, if I so much as miss a breath being on time to the office is out of the question.

I have become obsessed with chasing time; red lights have become my friends. On any given day, I'm running behind a mode of transportation that has an engine, the moment a traffic signal turns into a countdown my anxiety level goes on the rise and I haul ass. Like my fellow commuting New Yorkers, I am at the mercy of New York City's MTA system, so being late was common. To be a New Yorker is to be on a constant countdown that turns into being at a high level of anxiety and stress on the verge of a meltdown or feeling accomplished, triumphant, and overall badass. We are a rare breed.

Normally, when I arrive at the office, I am a sweating hot mess running late. Why is it that I never really feel like I am completely prepared?

My hair is pretty much always in a bun and always losing its hold, indicative of my life, my skirt is too tight, my heels aren't built to run a marathon across NYC, and as I race by all the retail stores in midtown looking at myself in their reflection my face sometimes looks like I am suffering from constipation.

Smile. Breathe. Slow down. To tell my lungs to breathe deeply, to bring in the breath, to hold it at my diaphragm, to bring oxygen into my physical being, to release and hollow out my stomach was an exercise I practiced every day. It is continual and deliberate. This marathon life and all its moving pieces will snatch your life like it will snatch your breath.

Coffee is just as essential! As a baby, Abuela would give me café con leche in my bottle and so my love affair with coffee has been lifelong. I am an avid coffee drinker and Starbucks is my dirty little addiction.

I'm going to tell you something about predictions. If Starbucks screws up your first cup of energy, you could chalk up the day to a loss. It's over. Therefore, your Starbucks morning crew is a lifeline, be kind, they have the whole world in their hands, well at least the first half of the day.

They know my fuel of choice, they know my name, I swipe, they put my name on a cup of Grande joy and the day has begun. Starbucks and even breathing. Some days that's chill mode. Some days that's all you get. The first sip of your coffee and the immediate inhale that comes after it. Relish it.

Woman Don't Cry

What a day!

Day so draining that whatever energy you have left is on autopilot, automatically the feet take you home, your brain in a daze, your heart at a slow thud, and your brain fried. I walked down the subway steps and observed a little boy, around 5 (he reminded me of Peter at that age although he was sitting, he had energy bouncing off his skin, and he was restless), sitting alongside a woman who was hunched over a bundle crying, she held a baby, 2 months old if that, the three of them sat on the dirty subway stairs of the orange MTA line, tired and looking beaten.

I remember this day as being very challenging for me, I cried tears of self-pity (not normally like me but no judgment).

As a New Yorker, I am desensitized to the city's fast-paced lifestyle and its begging, homeless, hustlers. Although, at that very moment the lady sitting on the subway steps raised her eyes from crying on her baby and looked directly at me. Her suffering resonated with me.

What I write about, what I stand in, for all that I have been, done, and been through faith and knowing that there is a reason for everything, love of life, and its Universal place in the world has gotten me to this point in my life. I am blessed!

Our eyes connected and I asked, "You, ok?" Her response was resolute, "Yes I'm ok." And I just knew she was going to be ok I knew this deep in my core. I then asked, "Do you have a place to stay?" She said, "Yes, a shelter." If you know me you know that if her answer had been no, I would have sat on those steps with her going through all my contacts to find a place and if that had not worked, I would have taken her and them babies home with me.

I looked down at that new baby and being a mother myself I knew that if I put my nose in the fold of her neck, she would smell like talcum powder and sweet baby sweat, if I put my finger in her tiny fist, she would squeeze it. I looked at the little guy and knew he wanted to run, stretch his little legs, jump up and down, and release all his little energy.

I shifted my gaze and looked at her and saw the pain of life, how she rocked her baby, for comfort, not to comfort the baby but to comfort herself. I nodded and swallowed the lump in my throat, took out money enough for pampers, formula, or dinner, if she needed them, gave her my card scribbled my cell # and said, "Call me if you need help".

Big tears rolled down her face from suffering swollen eyes, my own eyes watered as well, and I thought "I have never been on these streets barely living; homeless" I whispered "Thank you" into the Universe shook off the self-pity and stepped into Spirit.

Fortunately, I have always been surrounded by love and support from my circle of influence. I'm not alone. Signs are posted everywhere in various manners to remind us of how blessed we are in comparison to the lives of others. How we recognize them and connect to Source is part of our evolution.

I have connected to my Creator with light and love, in bliss, love is at my core. At that very moment I connected to that love on the dirty steps of a NYC subway, and I was given a lesson in perspective.

Spirit lives in all of us and there are those of us who carry more suffering as a testimony to those of us who carry less. For whatever circumstances that woman might have been through to put her on those subway steps with her children she served as a lesson to me, and I honor her.

I am not an I Do

Dedicated to the revolving door of the temporarily resurrected Men.

I wasn't meant to marry you. I'm sorry. I wasted an "I do" and now it's done. I was tired of the fanciful love – heavy on passion – head in cloud - butterflies in stomach – revolving door of "in love" relationships. So, I settled. I settled for monotony and a one-dimensional life. Flat. What did it matter that there was no spirituality involved? This was not a covenant.

Your deer-in-the-headlights reaction to my art was trivial. My manuscript became a reference, a guide of patterns and cycles that you started to dissect.

Could I live with an ear that could not tell the difference between Biggie and Tupac, West Coast and East Coast, whose head did not automatically bop; vibe- nonexistent? This was not a 90's R&B love affair and Lyfe Jennings did not live here nor did his Someone. Someone to understand? Must be nice.

And when I asked you what your purpose was you could not even begin to know the definition of it although you had sowed life. So, I subtracted my Oneness and zeroed out my connection. Threw up the "Do not swim in this area – Depth is too much to handle" sign.

When I asked you, what made you proud to be Boricua. You gagged. The ink on your skin branded into the brown flesh of your arm outlining our Puerto Rican flag spoke nothing to the gag order of the 1950s and Revolution; Pedro Albizu Campos was not even a name in your registry. Anacaona was a song you danced Salsa to not the Taina Queen that was howling hypocrisy from the depths of my center – La India de raza cautiva. You, who grew up alongside palm trees at the foot of the Rio Grande. Could not defend your pride against my offended Brooklyn-born hybrid Nuyorican sensibilities. While you were surrounded by her abundance I fed on the bread and water of the concrete jungle, bastardized, for being born en los Estados.

What did it matter? Surely, I could tamper down on the Wild Thing that had lived her life by the seat of her pants populating the world without a care in the world as if this living in the natural was the most natural thing to do. As if a century ago, she hadn't walked the earth barefoot, majestically wild, and burned at the stake for it. And still, she gave birth to her soulmates. And still, she brought forth life. And still, she was judged and persecuted. And still, a century later she would seek to hide in the grey areas of matter as if her legacy did not matter. She said I do in monotones and settled. Do you Fulano De Tal take this Wombman to be your lawfully... No! No! No! NOOOO!!.... We must re-write these vows. For better or worse? Through sickness and in health, till death do you part? What if I had experienced death already? What if every time I had stepped onto this altar, I had sacrificed portions of my soul for the sake of settling? Ritual. Ceremony. Trabajo.

Do you woman promise to...

No!!! Wait a minute!

How could I possibly keep vows in monotone when my incantations are vibrations that cannot be heard, nor seen but felt? I come in dreams and speak in tongues. I've given birth to Myself. I am Bruja. My love is magic, and magic is a gift that calls to be shared. This is my purpose to embrace my essence wholeheartedly connecting with the Devine Mother – I am not an I do – I am an I am.

Purge

I threw away our sheets today.

Where once your arms laid me to rest.

Now, the fabric and all its fibers wrap me in memories that carry me into unfulfilled dreams.

I threw away our sheets today.

They were calling for you at dawn asking why your side was cold.

You didn't answer them. As I pulled them from the corners and wrapped them up with all our memories they screamed in agony.

Is throwing something away the same as walking away?

The sheets want to know.

Death of a Soulmate

It doesn't matter how much time has passed, certain reminisces will kick your ass.

I have known poisonous love, love so toxic that I have lost the love of myself to love another. It would be that love that put me on a path of discovery, on a path of death, mourning, and realization.

Normally I do my self-reflection at night, it's when I connect with my home and its pulse, check in with life, my life.

Some nights are echoes that run like black and white silents. On this night, I watched a woman crying and her whole body shook from the sobs like an addict kicking a habit. In truth, she was detoxing poisonous love.

Love may be the worst type of addiction, and perhaps the strongest motivator within human nature.

The search for love, too much love, validating love, the love of money, the love of power, and the lack of love will move you to heights that if you are not careful will have you fall into an abyss.

I watched this woman in the reel of life, surrounded by darkness, a room in shadows her bed her sacrificial altar where she was dying a soulful death. Tears like rivers overflowed into her mouth because she could not close her lips from the silent screams of pain, agony, and betrayal.

Rocking herself, arms hugging her heart trying to keep some of what she still had, knowing that it was seeping out through her tears, through her silent cries, death was slow for it had been a long love.

Her chest heaved as unseen forces were ripping her very essence from her heart, and the pain of it would bring to bear a fresh new wave of tears, hugging her knees into her chest burying her face within her very center, the gravity of pain so profound that it pulled her into herself.

Her hair was wet, salty, and sweaty on her face, a blanket of it covered her, she blended into the shadows, and you could barely make out her profile. In a night of "Well we will just have to wait and see if she makes it through," in a fight for her very heart, I watched as love died the death of a soulmate.

Love's betrayal would take with it her light leaving her empty and dark. Cold.

She would survive the night; it would take a very long time for trust and love to find her again.

That woman was me.

Broken Women Syndrome

I can be any number of broken women I know. Cut their teeth on liberation and shackled domestication. Incubating conflicting paradigms and nurturing self-hate. C-section woman. Laboring under stress and failure to progress.

I can be any number of broken women I know. Growing faster than they could shed skin. Chafed. Dry. A brittle cynical broken woman. Self-deprived - having fed a generation of self-entitled love.

I can be any number of broken women I know. Love so hard that we break ourselves to keep a heart whole - even if it's not ours. A depleted broken woman. Givers and Laborers.

I can be any number of broken women I know. "Too strong," they say. "Too bold," they say. Possessed too many of the traits that my foremothers were too afraid to demonstrate. I breached a toxic womb - A Day One Darwin Daughter - adapting to an ever-changing landscape - proving that only the strong survive.

I can be any number of broken women that I know. But I'm not.

Affirmate!

>To all those things that have tried to destroy me:
>I am still here!
>Faithfully,
>Una Luchadora

It takes a special kind of understanding to love beautiful broken women. I share this because you can look at us from the outside and not see the battles that rage or the heartache we carry.

Especially those of us who practice kindness, gratefulness, and an optimistic mindset, those of us who continually work on focusing our attention on the positive because we genuinely are knee-deep in the work of bringing about change and not just complaining about our circumstances.

I am positive and productive while still dealing with hurt and pain, I am actively working on not allowing those emotions to consume me or feeling like a buster for putting on the happy face when inside I'm falling apart.

I've had to break off pieces of myself to become whole, a shattered mold.

Nothing we do to rectify our lives that puts us on a path to a better SELF is small. Small steps lead to BIG things.

Remnants of Seed

The Woman of Apocalypse (Wild Woman), the Dragon, and the Seed - Book of Revelation.

In the book of Revelation, the Dragon never wavered in his attack on the woman, even after the promise was delivered. Here we are women, thinking that it's what we deliver into the world that is to be devoured and so we protect that the most.

What we deliver is what we multiply and that can signify almost anything we touch and most noted are our children, careers, voice, and/or purpose.

The Dragon continually attacks the woman.

Why? Because we are the remnants of seed!

Definition of remnants - a surviving trace!

The seeds of purpose are in women and that is what must be protected. Give a woman anything and she will multiply it! Now multiply a promise to humanity. Abundance is female.

Instinctively, I have always referred to myself as a wild woman. It wasn't until I heard a sermon referencing the wild woman during personal development that I realized why. I have at every moment of my life been steered into the wilderness, an inhospitable place, and yet flourished.

There are so many more dragons to slay, purpose to deliver, and layers to heal. And so, let it be as the Wild Woman of The Apocalypse that slays the Dragon protecting the seeds of hope and promise.

I am that Woman

Somewhere in the world, there's some woman who is finding different things wrong with herself.

Me, I'm that woman.

The post-pregnancy belly will never go away no matter how many ab exercises I do.

Arms are too big.

Hips too wide

Hair is either too frizzy or too oily.

Sharp nose

I can continue to add to this list like nails in a coffin of my self-execution.

I have been at a healthy weight and still found fault with myself, just as much as I have found fault with myself when overweight.

The disfiguring of my body is not a result of the weight on my person but of the lack of love and acceptance of Self during all the different stages that reflect the numbers.

While I work on my physical goals, I am in complete acknowledgment that I must work on my mental and emotional endurance.

These arms have been raised and lifted for generations! They are STRONG!

The loose skin on my belly stretched from time and space. It became the Universe for living breathing human beings!

My hips stretched to accommodate life and gave me the ability to labor in pain.

My hair represents two of three races in my DNA, Africana y Taina! Ashe!

My European Spanish Arabic aristocratic nose is uppity, soy conquistadora! Allahu Akbar.

This inner struggle is one I know I am not alone in.

Somewhere in the world, there's some woman who is finding different reasons why she should love herself.

The strongest love is the love that can demonstrate its fragility. We get to hold each other up.

CreateHer

LoveHer

Meditate and Masturbate - the same hand you pray with - play with; both acts are sacred.

He wants to have his cake and eat it too, but she is Pi. Infinite.

While he may never starve, he will be unable to finish. Gluttony is a sin, but cleanliness is next to godliness, clean your plate.

She will cum for him with no strings attached, a broken marionette.

TravelHer

You are not a tourist attraction, a sightseeing point of interest to be checked off some bucket list!

No, Diosa.

You are the pull to a destination, a far-off land that draws at the very soul of a person.

A quiet beach at midnight with sands that reflect the full moon surrounded by onyx ocean and whispering waves.

You are the shelter of a cave at the false summit of a cold hard mountain after a deliberate climb.

You are the scent of wild lavender and pungent earth. A wondrous trek of self-discovery; guided sunbeam tour through majestic woods.

A haunting DcJa'Vu in the subconscious awakened REM. Fleeting and alluring.

You are a place of belonging they can't stay in.

The Nerve of Her – Clit * Oh * Hiss

Come, let me talk into your mouth while I suckle on my drippings, licking your glazed-over lips, after I have emptied my desire into your mouth from the slit of my clit. I crave nothing more than an endless supply of moments that have me whispering a secretion-infused saliva plea of "Put it in".

His kisses taste of folly, fuckery, and the bread of life. I am in search of sinful salvation. My body, a ceremonial slab of soft flesh and dry clay; a surface that swallowed death and delivered evolution. Is this what they mean when they say born again? Because I've died a million times with him, yet I have never felt more alive.

GossipHer

If these walls could talk, they'd say you read in braille and speak with a slow drawl - annunciating every hiss - my name spoken word while your fingers unroll sacred scroll - this skin parchment paper - a fragile doctrine.

If these walls could talk

They'd misinterpret biting lips and smothered gasps - How does one articulate a tongue in the throes of love?!

If these walls could talk

They'd plead to be released from the agony of deafening screams and the torture of witnessing a death that peals away the layers of paint and mortar baring heart-heavy crawl spaces where my orgasms echo and bounce off wood beams - we are all haunted.

If these walls could talk

They'd say you've made a temple of my body - and they witness nightly ritual.

Spirited Righter

There are stages to this, some days it feels like I'm just chasing my tail until I realize the circumference of the vision I've created for myself has expanded.

It's a marathon, not a sprint.

All of it is material. This is what I teach my kids. No losses, all lessons. Take what you receive and apply it to the next experience.

There are experiences I can scratch off my vision board and say, "That was a success". While there are those experiences that I've had to fully concede to as being "fodder for the fire". Both are material in their respective ways and have been part of my becoming.

I won't hold on to things that deplete and drain me.

Reciprocity is the name of the game.

I have learned to let go of things that may seem to the naked eye as quitting when in fact it is restructuring. Fail forward!

I have learned to have patience and grace with myself because if I stay true to the woman I want to become all will be as it should be.

I was planted under the shade of a wise woman:

"Nena, tu eres una luchadora. Si tienes un pensamiento échalo por adelante lo demás es un cuento." - Abuela

I was raised a modern-day Matriarch a la cañona.

A decade ago looked like this;

Mom of four kids

Published my first book

Moved back from Tampa, Florida.

Today…

I am the mother of four kids (successful adults/young adults in their own right)

Grandmother
Published my second book
A successful career in corporate America
Created a brand and became an entrepreneur
Sold a business
Purchased and sold a house
Moved several times during a pandemic
Formed new friendships
Reinforced existing relationships
Expanding the circumference.

I think the thing that stands out the most is that I've had to breathe life into my dreams pretty much on my own. A touch of melancholy hits because building a legacy can sometimes feel lonely if not for all the amazing, wonderful people I've met during this journey.

In as much as I have poured myself into people, places, and things by doing so with an open heart - I have been blessed by the same.

And still, I am a work in progress.

Awakening can be a beast, especially if you're not ready!

Imagine having catalyst moments that come equipped with battery cables connected to Source ready to charge and change your life whether you want it or not.

You are not ready!

Becoming can sometimes look like a mess while still being beautifully catastrophic.

Full Goddess in bear mode being dragged out of hibernation. You are not a bear! Wake up! You are a spiritual Goddess! I thought I wasn't ready to do the WORK, so I slept and slept and slept! When in fact it was just my unwillingness to connect to my divine purpose and to embrace it wholeheartedly, with courage, with heart. I was scared! I was tired! Yet, unwittingly, I was doing the work.

"Courage is not the absence of fear but the assessment that something is more important than fear." (Franklin D. Roosevelt)

During this latter part of my journey, my awakening and becoming at times have felt like a sledgehammer to my armor, ripping away at my cocoon and breaking me wide open.

The birth of the progeny Matriarch was not pretty. By standards, I was too young to be thrust into an elder position but unwilling to allow the threads of family and love to fall adrift.

Family leaders are a lighthouse, they serve as a steadfast beckon of welcome and guidance.

This new but familiar role has been a falling into grace that has been intense. You cannot Photoshop this stage. I have hyperventilated on self-imposed responsibility, moving through different transitions, and losing elders while becoming a leader of my family and tribe. All the while evolving into different versions of myself.

It is a scary thing to love someone blindly while you are witnessing their growth, transforming into different versions of the person you first met. One of the bravest things we can do is to love familiar strangers. One of the bravest things we can do is to love the different versions of ourselves.

Everything I am supposed to be is bleeding through the creases of everything I have ever been.

There is a monumental shift taking place in my Life and I have been trying to restrain my experience of it by safely playing within these invisible boundaries, answering to contrary roles and their expectations.

As the main character of my life, I am the head of the house I hold for, soy cabeza. A Matriarch, a moral compass, who at times has been a broken clock.

A creative that must pay the bills with a 9-5 yet yearns to lose herself in the arts. A Woman that wants to be loved with abandon but supported with discipline. A Mother who is underappreciated but universally loved.

A Friend who cannot lend you money but will bankrupt her energetic field to keep you in the light. Always in service because ultimately leadership in action is love, and love in action is service.

Ascension is not a weightless thing for heavy is the head that bares the crown.

The responsibility of all these roles on most days feels like a weighted blanket, the benefits of which are immeasurable. Yet on rare days, I want to drop all the balls I'm juggling and lose all restraint. To love, fuck, and release all my inhibitions, screaming my release and foregoing the weight of leadership. Selfishly driven by my personal need to be loved and led.

It is through my practice that I have been able to master myself and not succumb to my baser instincts. To experience the experience, to have gathered enough of myself to have a library of resources to draw from. To have successfully navigated me out of chaos and crisis, to fulfill the promise of my purpose, no matter how painful the journey has been.

To wholeheartedly love me and fully reconcile the different versions of myself during my becoming, the hurt child, the wild woman, the spirited righter, the Matriarch.

About the Author

Jenning C. Medina is a Nuyorquina from Brooklyn, New York. Having lived in upstate New York she currently resides in the borough of Staten Island with her family and fur baby Lucy.

A single mother with a formal education in Business Applications. Jenning has worked extensively in Corporate America with a career as a C-Level Executive Assistant spanning over 25 years. An avid believer in holistic healing through energy work and its different modalities, righting (spelled intentionally this way) coupled with energy work has been her way of working through her life's traumas, choices, and lessons. Jenning has used the modality of creative writing and the events in her life to inspire thought-provoking dialogue, which she hopes resonates with the collective.

She is a football mom who enjoys music, dancing, socializing, and networking. With an extensive network in the arts, she has curated art exhibits while bringing various communities together. Co-host at 11220 The Show a podcast that lovingly pays homage to Sunset Park, Brooklyn where she was born and raised.

www.ingramcontent.com/pod-product-compliance
Lightning Source LLC
LaVergne TN
LVHW092056060526
838201LV00047B/1424